I0799672

Praise for

Mantras of the Moon

My favorite of Srijani's poems is At Haridwar Ghat. It captures a tiny moment in time, while also holding up to light monumental things such as longing, celebration, as well as loss. Each of the poems in this collection offers sensory delights. They also reveal a love for place and history, and a commitment to close observation not unlike the devotion of a disciple.

~ Sayantani Dasgupta, author, *Women Who Misbehave*

[Srijani Mitra's] poetry is a compelling sample of her insightful perceptions about the interplay between the universe of energy, and our human world of energy's manifestations into material forms. She captures how we connect the dots in the infinitely different ways that we grapple with ambiguity in our attempts to understand the meaning of our lives, and the purpose of our actions.

~ David Thibeault, author, *Made in California*

Mantras of the Moon

Red Rook Press

This is a work of fiction. Any references to actual persons, living or dead, events, or locales are used fictitiously

To request permissions, contact the publisher at redrookpress@gmail.com.

Paperback: 978-1-972259-00-9
eBook: 978-1-972259-02-3

First paperback edition May 2026

Cover design: Elizabeth Golembiewski
Table of Contents: Sam Brown

Printed by Mixam in the United States of America.

Red Rook Press
Box 870244
The University of Alabama
Tuscaloosa, AL 35487-0244

Mantras of the Moon

- POEMS

SRIJANI MITRA

Table of Contents

Author's Note

This poetry collection is deeply personal to me. Many poems weave in words from my mother tongue to express the cultural nuances of the place and heritage I belong to. These terms are not simply linguistic choices; they reflect the concepts, ideas, and images I grew up with, shaping the imagination that informs my writing.

I have made cultural and mythological references like Kochuri which is a beloved Bengali snack referenced in the poem "Residence." It evokes the familiar warmth and everyday joy of Bengali culture. I have mentioned Kali or the fierce goddess from Indian mythology in "Mermaid Myths, Reconstructed." She symbolizes an indomitable spirit and the destruction of evil which are qualities I deeply admire. I have used kundali in one of the poems to signify the vital energies of the spirit, a concept rooted in Indian spiritual traditions.

I love Indian philosophical concepts which is seen in my use of Rasa Theory which is central to Indian aesthetics, the Rasas or the eight core sentiments that shape emotional experience. I draw upon them in my poem "Of the Truth," reflecting my long-standing fascination with this theory.

I allude to Atman meaning "the soul," representing the essence of selfhood explored throughout the collection.

Chaitanya signifying "consciousness," is a recurring idea in poems that examine inner life and awareness.

Some poems have cultural objects in them like the Akashbati, central to my landscape and culture. I refer to beloyar or colourful glass traditionally used in chandeliers, included as a symbol of luminosity, ornamentation, and memory.

My long-standing love for psychology, supported by my academic background, influences many of the collection's themes. I use titles like Theories of Emotions and reference the idea of catharsis to connect poetic expression with psychological concepts I particularly enjoy.

These terms and ideas form the inner architecture of the collection. They reflect my understanding of Indian aesthetics, my ways of dreaming and thinking about culture, and my relationship with love, emotion, and selfhood. Together, they shape my poetic interpretation of the world which I essentially feel is raw, reflective, and deeply rooted in the traditions that have shaped me.

For my Grandmother and Late Grandfather

At the Haridwar Ghat (Har ki pauri, 2016)

It was fulgent, the whole of the place.
The day was Dussehra and there was celebration
Of the goodness triumphing, they say it's the day of burning the evil

Wiping off the maligned megrim—a renaissance, a resurrection, a joyous victory.
My sister and I stand at the narrow edge of the Ghat—a shade as a saving grace

For us away from all the loudness—the elders
Sip chai beside us and recall age old history
Restless of the forlorn sense even amid the lurid lights and boisterous burst of
Crackers like large gambolling fireflies,

Hovering around us,
We gradually sit by the sea—our bodies closer to it—regurgitating eternally

And carrying the tattered wastes with it in bits and pieces

Still as a distant sight we watch the fire

Of all the burning, baring everything
Glowing and rising like an inexorable spring

A kindled Diya comes floating through the skimming Ganges—reaches

All its way to us. My sister picks it up from the scrim of waters,

Adores it with her slender pink fingers and
    Palm and then she puts it back again within

The dark viscous waves
And that day

It was almost as if
We watched a tiny glimpse, really a span of time,

A momentous revelation eclipsed

Of how our lives and ribs would eventually shape,

Burning and dousing, taking in all the warmth to only, eventually

Give back to the silence of the river, ocean, sea.

Portrait in Adbhutam Bhava

And it is again making rounds,
Digging the grounds
Of sun-scarred hollows of
Memories
Muddy
With the dust spittoons
Buried in the old almirah haze,

A drawer solitary and numb like my ark of ribs
Wintry as disgruntled air of the bony whitewashed day.

I stumbled across the brown- tinged picture of my Grandpa
The other day.
Mustard,
Sepia in the neurosis of nostalgic times,
Marooned as that cold kohl- rimmed gaze in his eyes,
A Gestalt of convalescent husky ashen battalion
Of pasts befuddling the

Cranium in unanswered questions,
Yet these are memories that we cannot do without,

Tainting the bare blue morning in pinpricks of dew and hazel light,
Leaping on noon flight, skimming the silky surface of emotions
Curdled into a moss,
A largesse of sorrow—unbending, wounding and thorough,
And what else am I left to do than believe

In the portrait of past as wonder, and
Awaiting the blur of intangible hues, wiping away everything in

Rain and mist and rue,
And what else to sew than the abandoned knots of threads

Unfettered reminiscence,

Leaving in the devotional blight of awe,
This yearning deep and wild,
This yearning of returning.

After watching a romantic web series

Madly pondering upon my ideas of love
How will it occur—the amateur need of intertwining—
The absurd stargazing with friends—moon soaked, choked
With the weird suffocation of being undone.

How could a lover be met in the aftermath of rain and the fall of moon glow
In simultaneity with
The beating throb of a wet mud heart
The messengers of wind and first trampled rain-washed dust
Upholding the corners of starlight refracting through the hazy sight.
How could romantic fantasies ever be realized in the soft kissing
Recovery of warm selves on a chilled night,
When the moon feeds the bedazzled night and sea marinates,
Unendingly,
Until it reaches the open-mouthed ocean, forming the delta, silting through sand.
How could this slow thrill build and burn seamlessly in the perfect idealism,
Perforated with impervious cells of the soul as a resuscitation,
Melding the want of throat, caressing the ribs as the night unfolds.

Defence Mechanisms

There is a beauty in defending the ego
Attributing assumptions and coagulations of sorts
Like a gush of emotions unexplained, changed and

Converted into justifications by this wondrous brain leading to
Denials of all sorts so that this ego—floating at times or submerged,

like the Axis Mundi conquering midst the known and unknown.

The conscious, subconscious, and unconscious.
It begins with repression, like pressing every shade of
Inappropriate confessions in the whirling pot of the mind,

And then there is the grandeur of rationalizing effects
And causes in accord—
All finally as a concurrence of conflicts—

In sublimation and every Freudian interpretation
Diverge as fine lines of denial—deny this, deny that—

The psyche teetering on edges of tearing apart—
Disregarding what is left as the residue from everything repressed,

Forgetful enough to recapitulate,
Unravelling the tapestries of mysteries lying within this incredible persona.

Solitude

Sitting unabashed through the haze of the tattered edge of bramble and
Upturned sky of memory
In a hoary grail inching towards me like a snail, slowly yet smoothly
Along the granular trail of our ridden intangible foibles,
Tales languishing in ridges, ledger of cardboard and photo frame,
Burnished in the scent of cupboard smell, the last cauldron
Of bottled perfume like a hue
Of doused flame, reminding how there's nothing left—no life, no
Essence, of the gathered emotions of us, boxed in the galloping chest
And unflourishing zest of love.
I navigate through empty spaces, the bed sheet spread—scald
And rufous designs barely saying what we were not,
And this room echoing and filling in the
Gnashing sound of silence, of gloom,
Of the clumsy demanding despair
Rising like a spell over me in fumes, telling me, pressing its
Heavy cage against my breath, how lonesome we are, how
Solitude exists in emptiness, in structure and form.

Gestalt of Memories

It never deceives the cognition of yearning, churning in the sulphur empires of the soul,
Grizzled in the grassy lawn of memories, green, tarred, charcoaled.
It happens on days like these
When the air has the aftertaste of rain,
        The sky—chunks of sandalwood, and
        The heart a museum of unavoidable pain evoking in
A synergy of clustered emotions,
Raw, raw
Like the sudden sputter of blistering rain,
Memories scatter in the unknown angular slants of light,
Broken into uncountable pieces—beloyari, glass like yet joining,
Joining to fill in the dried ocean within,
To come together as wholesome integrity, charting

The iridescent vulnerabilities of the heart, to fill
The parched topology with the softening touch of warmth,
The endless resfeber, the converging path of the body, mind, heart,
Journeying, journeying.

Portrait with Victoria Memorial in view

We are huddled, placidly,
In the
Kolkata taxi,
The night breathes
Ocean purple sky
Changing its hues intermittently,
Our palate of throat,
Swallowing ruffles of nostalgic
Moonlight.
There is the
Fuzzy warmth,
Gentle mercy
Of molten love, juddering
As the noisy wind rattles outside.

The motion parallax as we pass the Victoria,
Moon lathered, soft-stoned, rose-grey, intensifies—the strange desire
Longing within.
I wonder
How I concocted dreams,
Dusted adolescent imageries
In the palm of this heritage,
Still sinking in,
Still tasting those fantasies into
Lost futures,
The ruddy animal
Of the chest gnawing,
Oh! What wilderness god,
Alas, heart,
A monumental alibi
In remembrance.

Portrait with Saraswati Puja and interrogations about Mantras

Saraswati Puja envelops the city
In vasant jewels—Shringaar spring,
Lush lavender days
Snake through vessels,
Slits and netsukes,
Paragon palettes, pulping past.
Morn splits ochre light pricks into succinct perforations,
Travelling morass, in devotion
Ribboned with ditsy deliberations, anamnesis glimpse.
I turn the mantra chanter today,
Traversing Vedantas, Ved,
Divined yantras
My unadulterated bhakti is never peripheral,
I hope,
At least the keeping of faith, it appears for me,
Is indeed secrecy—
The Padma eyes of Bishalakhhi,
Glistening in front of me,
Her mantle, her world—the conscious,
The jnana residing in the soothing, marble calm
Flare surrounding her—
She must recognise her bhaktas, and their endless demands,
Knowledge, the shakti to believe in that Chaitanya
Is what I conjecture,

I demand
In this grid,
This moment,
As I am muttering Mantras—sharp edged, flowered, offerings, Anjali,
And I question the integrity,
Within and externally, suddenly—
Wavering around the conflicting arousal
A wandering scurry,
I question the summoning of Vishnu in the mantra medley.
 It might be desperate to ask,
So in the Puja session,
Father pretends complete avoidance,
Sister reciprocates,
I know not what mother and grandmother
Would respond to this sudden euphoric assailing query,
But once I perceive,
Internally swallowing—
Submission,
Examination,
As syrup, juice, stern walled city
Inside,
Bhakti, Atman, Vidya
An insight
Do I percolate in the rock bottom soil?
The rooted rigidity scattering, rained essence,
Bhakti saying submission is integral, quintessentially mutual

Testimony, epiphany,

A perimeter protecting the personal Goddesses beyond.

The concentric concurrence,

Asteroids, sediments, floating spirit, sundry coils,

Sorted fumigate.

Do I visit the temple?
Town, the meditating dawn.

Of silence listening to the silence that originates from this brine.

This Samudra.

Roaring, revealing, salmagundi assorting.

Frames

And it is a Sunday afternoon,
Emptied out in a visage of sunny pink,
Molting like a faint memory shedding its iridescent skins.
There's a lofty emptiness peering from somewhere near my bedside.
It feels like a trail of huddled past cupped together in the lone, rattling through a portal

of flashbacks, nudging me into believing
All of those ashen bits of mucky dreams can be true.

I search the grand mound of framed photos in the ancient drawers,
Still breathing of Sunday brunches and picnics, morsels of hungering frantic quest for love.

The broken edges of friendships, smoky stuff,
Effervescent and glimmering in the gloaming, pigments of salwood remain.

Entering this cumbersome catacomb of the past
is never easy,
Engendering an unpredictable heightening of affects,
Carnal and pixelated—
Half-alive, half-unvisited in the kantha soft wisdom of heart,
Heaving the self to pains—growing,
Intangible,
To aches—unforgiving,

Returning, gathering, yet breaking

Every time

As desire,

As a feverish, incurable wounding of love.

On watching this rodomontade

In the voice of Shakuntala
And there are days when the mad heart turns brave,
With its arrhythmic beat stuttering in a monotonous way.
It wants to clutch onto something
Say
That something it beseeches itself to forget.

Someone somewhere lures you to ecstasies,
You are mistaken—you know,
Yet you turn raw
In the sputtering sense, soiled, mati stained, marinate
Over and over and over
Again.

You want to summon them and say
"Hey, hold me until I fall again,"
You want to traverse the rocky pathways, the granite mounts midst
Hushed breath
You want to sink in
And fill the hollows with the smoothened slime,
The sleek crystal waters
That gush by
You want to say how you feel
But you lie knee-deep, sodden,

Perforated with so many pauses like a poem.

You are afraid there is no coming back.

You are afraid

Of leaving.

You are afraid

It has never been so close with the earth. So close, that you could talk of separation.

You can only sit

Then

Wander

Taking in all the warmth that space could provide at that time and

Tell yourself to witness the self.

Know the now, be still, turn to

All the power greater than anything else

Feel the heavy thrumming beat,

Breathe.

Of the truth

When the truth shall visit us at the other end of the Ghat—
Bank of this river
Long, whooshing, splashing, laboriously lyrical.
How will it befall us? Will it be like
A mystic in orange robes—the Baul from the forestry of Bengal—
The Saint haloed with overripe lemon lights,
The gallery of Goddesses and gods, the whirling gowns of constant motion
And liberating emotions from tangling like moss,
Seeping in the undergrowth and pushing within
Like the weight of unbearable things—the crazy whirlwind of samsara.
Is this how truth would reach us,
As Tagore says, rising anew near the shores of Rupnarayan
Drowning, echoing, lilting, glowing in a newness—
An emancipation from wild enjambments,
To behold the beauty, the mystery, the essence of all rasas and hues
In that one split epiphany of time
Almost salving and blending, shading and enlightening
In heated hues of warmth—
Peach skin,
Cherry red,
Autumnal view—
Is it where God is found, God who is far away yet close here,
Very near,
Within me, yet I am without.

Is it where the fetus of every intrauterine hope rejuvenates itself
Splintering like colours of twilight cut and chiselled,
Collecting together again to remake.
Is that how we arrive at the truth, blooming like lotus,
Glowing in an inflammable expanse,
Diving into the luminosity of
Where the vigil ceases and the last light of the world
Like cradling arms, directs you to the will of this spinning universe,
To the swish of silence,
At the other end of the Ghat?

In a Murshidabad Museum

We grab the happy holidays, lattice the strings, energize ourselves to better glories

Not affording anything without our will
As the long stretches of green land seem Godhuli lit
From a distance, and a mild tremor is felt in the ribs.

An anxious recovery from the past and frill of emotions circumscribes us.

Sister stands in front of an old photo glistening in Sand drizzle scenes.

Amniotic ambience
In the spice mist of moment everything seems unpredictable.

Shadowed

She is here,

Close to the lattices.

Drowning even though she has known

The penchant,

The Matope, the grown fangs, fatal fevered desire

To fly.

She grabs the mesh, mush crimson blood laced dress, holds onto it, and cries.

Asks for a song to sing, a word, or some form, a thing as soft as a pillow, as warm as a bonfire

Chiselled out of her bare bones

So that she might know what to make of this. This moment.

How to tame her demanding frottage when she wants

To live in this space yet again.

She collapses into empty makeshift houses,

Softly whimpers like a street unborn in the morning city,

Like a whitewashed grief in unending longing

Her shadow is indistinguishable from what she has become.

She wants to be, from where she lives and where from she emerges every single day

Powerless and powerful she indulges,

Takes strings, warp and weft in cussed anamnesis

Climbs up and down

The rocky labyrinth,

And lays all her tales

In front of me.

My eyes smoked with fear, detonating poppy bluish wrath mirroring somewhere

That bashes my empty breath

So much as I can't look through, I am unable to see

As the barrenness rushes into whirling fields,

As the September drizzles over

As if it is a throat satiated in the monsoon,

As the ground and sky,

And roof of life build

Their own communions

In the transit.

Lost in Murshidabad

Hazarduari glistens as we traverse round and round the arena.

Flowerets on the ground seem like meenakaris laid as jewellery from ancient palaces.

My sister glimmers with a finesse,
Mother and father recapitulate their love story,
The museum enlightens in the bustling cacophony

Hours of roaming.

The Imambara's closed doors stand tall as we build small mounds of memories
With sleek vision,

Teeming in viscosity our day alights
On a different note tuning to a familial love,
A warmth that I witnessed after a long time,

An unconditional love embalming us in the middle of history.

On Saraswati Pujo, 2022

Again, flashing lights

Dimming skies

Recurrence recurrent repetitive

Grudges

I say

Fuck you.

Remember an excuse me

I say. I hate you

Remember spewed lies.

Believe me?

I say the entire world is so beautiful, so paint me in orange hues,

So dance like Kamla Sundari with her dotara rising to a timbre so attuned that

We wander wander in wonder

Staring upwards, startled at the skyward leap, enjoying bits of splashed episodes

Sliced apart apiece.

Say cool, say ice tea, say milk-washed sundae

I love it all

I love this story, this story, this story of you and me.

Dream light

Someone spews something in the kitchen, sun spilling out of the window like an orange lamp laid in front of the cornea

The clayey viscosity of the day pulls me up and calmly says how I love the wooden enjambments of it

How the road narrows down into something small and gripping

How love becomes diademed yet hollowed out like a moksha, not yet defined

Not attained

The altitude of the body reaches as the cage heaves dust foam evokes like spittoons from matter molten in the skyline

The parabola light entwines wisps of words like domes in Murshidabad, and the solitude seems contagious

Corroding/effervescent/efficient/glistening/luminescent/grotesque

And I slip in the uncanny boughs

Rajnigandha scent suffocating me with words of beauty

Galvanisation corruption hallucination

And I say I want nothing to stay as time scatters away

I say I want the calm safety of beds the woollen wealth of life, the smitten dream of sense bound in a perfect circumference towards a holy stained sight.

Monsoon of Memories

Between the echo of receding past
and

The plunging plasma of current
is

The secret sub-periphery of memories.

Sprinkling like light dust, opaque, yet translucent enough

To cut and fold and arrive unexpectedly as flashbulbs.

How this suddenness feels like a throaty lump, unavoidably numb

How it waxes sour deep in the moon's scarred, burnt epidermis, how it

Reinvents forms of verging the past—the oldest arts of brutish love, the

Raw emulsification into a stormy roar of raging times.

In the end, there's no respite other than seeping into the taproots of

Moments diverging into straggling filaments of recall,

All strewn over the lush woodlands, hidden and scrubbed.

This is the time when we make of what

Remains

Floating boats of paper-thin size,

As the thump transmutes into a singsong adieu,

A euphoric scooping out of

The sewage of a remembering decay.

Residence

I reside on a riverine land,

An eastern side of subcontinental dreams and embracing Bengali beams.

Here's the cradling city I live in—a plunge pool of perspiring history and a

Crisscross of skylight entering the canopy of our bushy, woody lives like a prismatic,

Lunatic silvered refracting light.

A city breathing flavoured history through its rusted lungs, congested chests,

A city Byzantine with its oli golis winding as mangy mazes in tetul twilight.

City greened with cheering grass of Maidan siesta light,

City bruised and blazed in an oceanic spur like the porous ends

Of how Bengali gossip ends.

A peripatetic city, a placidly implacable city,

A city of grand celebration, chanting incantation,

Crackling with laughter when the Howrah Bridge slumbers

With the incandescent bright of godhuli.

Scrubbed white city like lime-washed churchyards

Of St. Thomas' Cathedral.

City of Goddesses emerging with ten hands

And shakti in the melody of ecstasy,

A city where I recall, reminisce, reclaim, redefine a finer fleecy silken thread of belonging,

Only to feel more convoluted in the cusp of its clasping topology,

City flavoured flamboyantly in the fuchka delight

And crispness of kochuri,

And the purer simpler smell of mati.

City that keeps singing mellow dissolving notes in the breezy wind of day,

City inscribed in the cavalcade of reverberation and emotion brimming as the heart and mind of Tagore.

Amritsar—safar

It always feels ethereal to be part of a beautiful story,

lying somewhere within the history of a town, as breathtakingly

Gorgeous as Amritsar. Amrit meaning the immortal, the elixir—it seems

The city has devoured all the liveliness, the amrit mystery of life, embedded in

Its memory, the soft reverberation of it chaotic charm. Ameristar glistens in the twilight

As we leave our sandals huddled in the grand Golden Temple courtyard. Then

Put aside all the buzzing sounds, entering the sanctity of the destination, the God.

I never experienced peace to be so tangible before, I could hold the day as it was

Blossoming above midst where the horizon met the sky rise temple—gilded, bright, I could

Open the curtained windows within to wander along the winding wisdom of Lord.

As we reached the heart of Amritsar, arteries of sweet air, the welkin just the colour of halwa

As a foggy dust of pink yawned at us, and the city cradled us, journeying, accumulating the

Lost segments of us, that we found again in this cusp, this recognition of Hiraeth,

Home.

Jwalamukhi Temple, 2019

It was almost twilight as the hue of the incandescent third eye of the Goddess and the fire that glows—purer, brighter, rising till eternity, in the sanctum of the temple—eclipsed in wonder, searing in the blessing of devotion, brimming with thousands of pilgrims each day. After the Darshan, we sat near the milky staircase on the cusp of the twilight song fulgent and embedding us in the roiling mystery of this divine world, pondering only if it was that God travelled to us on such a dusky flight, graciously sweeping the darkness aside, as the spiralling rings of smoke fill the sphere of life, from the evening Aarti, is it how the light of the world evolves, tearing apart the blood-red sky, bisecting our parched atria, and filling our porous, mud-filled, thirsty bruises of self in diademed glory, conscience and love like a lightened dome of our hearts, is that how we find God? In us, defenestrating the rusted wounding despair out of the frame, and knowing again where the ocean accumulates in form, where the fire blazes iridescent as dawn.

On studying theories of emotion

I am haunted by its conquest,
How the animality in this emotion tinges me red,
Turns my lust
Like scattered petals, pulping enzymes
In refracting,
Recurrent rain.
Today, we are diving into
The anatomy of emotions, which is to say
The exactitude that moves us,
How the stimulus information
Triggers physiological reactions
Leading to exclusive emotions
Birthed at the crown of the thalamus, communicated by the cortex—

I wonder how this can possibly justify my arousal—
How I let my frame of bones squash in the rinsing
Overwhelm at the shower,
How the collection of water about my blue nerves,
The hollow sweat-embalmed nape, the kundali of my navel,
The fulcrum fecund feeling in the bosom, grows
At the perception of your touch.
The tactile, decayed celebration of bodies breaking through
The paradigms, clasping onto each other, to extract
The nectarine lilies, the succulent passage within life, how can I

Interpret this emotion, wound by logic or molten desires
As grazing mouth in the field of honeyed acacia, in
The soft pulsating yearning of your tongue, rimmed
With sugar, syrup, spirited thrum.
Continued,
How might I branch out these emotions to classify
Them as limbic understanding, the simplified cortex sensation,
How could I expect its consequences to affect my body,
In its drowned existence fisting onto uprooted pleasures
Like ocean silk shards greasing the epidermis with healing.

Knowledge of the body

Listening to lectures on the body's pleasure, excavating the mounds in historiography
Of expressing sexuality,
Kama Sutra, lasya, and pleasures,
I realize
How all these years I had wronged my body to believe in its kinetic presence,
In blundering. Now that I desire to know its evolution,
To strip the skin off the ribs and peer at its striking beginnings,
Strings, ribboned membrane sheaths, cell sap
Eschewed codes merging into lotusing, arising.
I want to flourish
In its writhing extravagance, the
Fire
Ignited in the edged spine
Transmitting something vast upwards
Towards the mind seated in the navigating essence,
The Axis Mundi—chipped with emotions intertwined.

I want to tap the touching grain rough mucous
In longing, in aching arches and emblazoned geometries like
Pietra dura sculpted over the body, dorsal portraits containing
Warbling mothballs, waters turning into smoked demands, wet porous fumes.
Oh lord turn me pilgrim, douse the flame filled onusondhitsha,
This lustrous rigour in the veins, setting everything to fire.

What I desire this summer day

All night, there has been such broiling,
Such pouring out—grinding geologies erupting with steaming zest.

This summer day seems a fest—all wild bewilderment,
Asphalt ridges in the sky slowly kissing the dawn,

The way desire smelts into something lighting,

Like fire. This summer day,

I want the safety of your breath, soft
Blooming blueness of skins blemishing

In touch, in thrill, in wildfire.

I want the honey winds to fill the lungs in a flurry,
Adorning its braziers with grace and briar.

I want taste, I want the drizzling thrum of transformation,
The expansive plunge into some stimulus, sense,

Sure—sensation

That I have longed for forever.

Mermaid myths—Reconstructed

Mami Wata (the African Mermaid)—Goddess of the African waters, nourishing the Shringaar green offspring of nature spread over the blue frescoes of seabed. She arises as the saviour, the mother in the cusp of bluish-green Shakti reclaiming the identity of her children with diamond-embossed charcoal skin. She arises as light, as storm, the divine destination of the sacred seas towards resurrection, towards the Satori, incandescent.

Suvanamachha (the Asian Mermaid)—the golden mermaid from the oceans of Thailand, with glistening glitter in her eyes, blesses the universe with a gilded fortune of flight. A figure from the Ramayana, her pure love springs with Hanuman. She flowers harmony midst the ocean folk and sweeps away their bottled up morose as a healing, embalming path towards faith.

Merrow (the Irish Mermaid)—her foamy fertile tresses—aureoled as spring—green

Twirl in the Irish waters—serene,

She rummages through the tides, harsh, to explore the halo within.

Selkie (the Scottish Mermaid)—from the lap of Scotland's lavish riverine lands, she appears as half-seal, half-human. Transforming as variegated hues of a kaleidoscope, the Gaelic maighdean-mhara fills the darkened spaces of mucky ravines with a bouquet of wonder and hope.

Melusine (the Medieval European Mermaid)—she reaches the shore as vengeance, as wrath like Kali in ruddy ire. Yet she appears in dreams, scaling winged fantasies in the gossamer flurry of imaginations, with a serpent tail and free pinions of pride, breathing of emancipation, the untameable, invincible strength of liberation.

Dream Islands

The night swings swiftly in the jingles of the evening bells from home's temples,
I slip aside into the ambiguous agony of the concrete, deciduous Lane—
Into the vanity of residual rain in puddles of memory.
A grand sight, visceral purity and glimpse
Of a blanketed, deepening sky as an unfolding plankton of sooty ocean
Narrating our beginning in the rutting realizations of teenage destinations—
Thriving in the clumsiness of a twitching touch of past lives—
I spread the sheets, there's a silence outside my window turning a blinking pink
From the Akash Bati's glittering light.
Here and there a bulbous flicker burns and hardens cliff-like, granite,
And I fall away from all this, as I say how much I really loved you—
As I say I somehow still love you—in this scattering,
Breaking yet clotting in the lap of the winged satins of night.
I faint and stay in a dreamy paint, an incantation in the body—
It feels as if we are together again.
I become an island, waters everywhere,
Corals surrounding my senses.
The secrets of love whispered in the rooms of my body
As Matsyakanyas dancing through memories,
Ripples touching the nubs of my thighs, pirouetting their way,
The gushing waters taking my breath away, I lie—
Bared open, open—Mawed, drinking water till the brink,
The sweetened honey stain in your body of fire—watering,
I lie muzzled in solitude,
Awake, healing, throbbing, intertwined.

Self-portrait as ocean bed

I am afraid of such nights, dimming skies

Burrowing as an open wound, I never know how this happens,
transforming the self, mud-soaked,

Tainted, stained with green beads, sea plants, fists of grassy shards of
time hollowed in the belly of an ocean.

I lie, drowned and flattened in the spread, water above, a deep
longing beneath, battering the senses into surrendering.

There is life; there is an unknown darkness brushing by as strokes of
ravaged remembrances.

I am refaced again; I know nothing other than the shelled pearls,
schools of mustard fish, a wavering mass of wonder and creatures,

All in the galloping waves, bruising and healing, stilling and parting,
as the shattered crystal pieces of ruined love.

Alien Skin

How is it, this chalky enmeshed wisdom of bones, like
A wintry rigidity, feels slushy with its cage at times.
This body prying
Open like a treasure trove on some days,
In half-shade, half-shelter,
A real alignment

Yet abruptly changing form,
Becoming unknown, unveiled—
Alien skinned,
Non-aligned
When I yearn for affiliation.

How is it when
I seek refuge, it's comforting, at times blooming like
A Lotus in a Godly land,
Welcoming into the core, really chanting something.
Mantras of devotion,
Echoes of the being called God.

On visiting Indian museum

Five of us friends delve in the beauty of the postcolonial charm

Singing odes to the beauty that is the Varaha, startled at the photographic charisma of the grassy lawn and mesmerised by the shalabhanjikas inviting us to the Bharhut complex we look with mouths open at the Egyptian marvels like we are time travellers

Carefree wind and the daylight paint us azure as we roam from room to room staring with starry eyes at paintings of hamams and harems and golden coins

As we bid farewell and dusk falls we hold the day close to our hearts so close so close as to never forget our friendships flowering midst this

Arching glory.

To be a little late, always

There's no known end to procrastination, and the unrestrained imagination,

Travelling far-flung

Out of wooden doorway frames, trapping the winds,

The scented, jasmine-rinsed skin of the cooling zephyr

Of a mildly molten day,

Trying to capture the light, the fleece of levity in corners of dusk—yellowed and grey.

As the saying is—you can never say, you will winnow tomorrow, *

But how can the heart not leap into

Thinking—how it is like to be always, a little late,

To be grimly twisted and to awaken

To inferences afterwards, when the pain has stashed itself to the ground as

Suspended dust, and

Down the lane of life where the conclusion thrives

Like the plaque of rust on old wardrobes—

The realisation creaks as a sleek, slow repentance,

Why is it yet so assuring to be slipping away as playing hooky,

To play the absentee, the one always arriving late.

*Chowdaiah of Ferrymen

Self-portrait as Navigating consciousness

After deep-delving conversations

We are dreaming the fetish, to be wholesome, to grasp things together,

Piecemeal, not smitten by delirium or defences

We are weaving cocoons that are safe, warm finesse,

Which is to say, there are spools of abandoned threads

 That demand association,

And midst the test anxieties

We hold the creaking visages—of light with our fingers

Our friend indulges in curiosities—abysmal, uncanny

Everything can't be known of the heart—it is indeed a dangerous space,

I collect unforeseen realities, visualise them in pink phosphenes,

Preconscious, subconscious deliquefies,

Fades in, facets of incomprehensibility

What remains is the dust from heaps,

postcards to the nebulae settling within us

They are rupturing other paradigms,

Politics, primeval states, walled grounds

Vasant charms vehemently, as I give in to this intersection,

As an immense froth, fulcrum of demands

The swishing silence dissolving everything

Springs

Such springs ravish as starring light, glaucous blemishes

A sudden recall of times

When I, in the peak of girlhood, rested amidst

The maidan panorama, extravagant body,

Greened burst—light ecstasy

How the honey sun light swayed,

How I gripped the ground as we housed love

In the caged animals. The heart.

The spring flashback vanishes every time in

This, like this, a soul vagabondness firing within

And a voice within—even though I am a woman now,

Still the same, in searching this way, this ambush

Of love, this veined sand bristling for

Some taste in the pink of tongue

Acknowledgements

Immense gratitude and love for everyone who has supported me in my writing journey, my family members, my partner, Rajdeep, for his constant support of my work.

Heartfelt gratitude to the following publications where some of the poems appeared—

Chautauqua journal, Propertius Press anthology, Mekong Review, Audacity Magazine, South Seattle Emerald, Mermaids Monthly, Frame zine, South End Stories

About the Author

Srijani Mitra is a writer based in India with works published in *North Dakota Quarterly, ItGetsBetter, South Seattle Emerald* and *Indian Literature* by Sahitya Akademi. She has spoken at Mangalore Lit Fest and Shoolini literary festival. She has conducted workshops across universities and colleges of India including IIT Guwahati and IIT Dharwad. Her website is srijanimitra.com.

Red Rook Staff

Red Rook Press is a student-run literary press from the University of Alabama

Acquisitions

Oliver LaRose (liaison), Alex Demuth, Charlotte Diel, Richard Dixon, Malik (Karsten) Erskine, Brea Gaillard, Kaira Harper, James Huntley, Scarlet Jacobson, Isa Matson, Aidyn McKinney, Marshall McGahey, Megan Millar, Mia Mittag, Ainslee Monroe, Nathan Neugebauer, Veronica Oehlers, Ava Rudd, Cooper Smith, Scarlet Sodergren, Ellie Spohrer, Kiley Stevens, Saadat Tayyibah, Alyssa Wallner, Mae Webster, Maggie Welch, Madelyn Woods

Audio

McKenzie Knight (liaison), Alex Demuth, Joie Ingram, Ava Rudd, Vaughn Taylor

Design

Anna Cobb (liaison), Anna Luis (liaison), Sam Brown, MiKayla Davis, Elizabeth Golembiewski, Andrew Kelley, Adyson Keough, Karliegh Plank

Poetry Editing

Jane Champ-O'Connell (liaison), Aaron Hightower (liaison), Aubrey Case (liaison), Victoria Bell, Lilli Davis, Malik Erskine, Brea Gaillard, Scarlet Jacobson, Ainslee Monroe, Skylar Small, Aidan Strebel, Reese Walker

Promotions

Maya Mungo (liaison), Sam Godwin, Kaira Harper, Adyson Keough, Dante Larkins, Megan Millar, Evelyn Moran, Tavetta Moton, Averi Obrien

Special Projects

Wrenley Brown (communications liaison), MiKayla Davis (children's book liaison), Livi King (P.R. liaison), Ever Wood (zine liaison), Jane Champ-O'Connell, Bee Hydrick, Dante Larkins, Mia Mittag, Aidan Strebel

Website

Ansel Smith (liaison), Jordan Earnest, Sam Godwin, Adyson Keough, Megan Millar, Tavetta Moon, Swastee Regmi, Saadat Tayyibah

Faculty Advisers

Paul Albano, TR Brady, Sarah Cheshire, Josh Dugat, Merrill Lee Girardeau, Stephanie Marker